Something Beautiful

Create your happiest, healthiest self,
and find the key to unlock
an extraordinary life.

COURTNEY ROBERTS

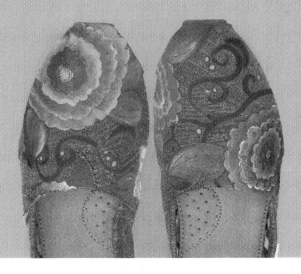

Something Beautiful

Create Your Happiest, Healthiest Self, and Find the Key to Unlock an Extraordinary Life

By Courtney Roberts

2

This book is dedicated to anyone who ever dreamed of living and extraordinary life, of finding something more. May you have the courage to step out of your comfort zone and enjoy the adventures that the world has to offer.

Table of Contents

Chapter 1: What Paul Gave Me

All of my life I have known that I was different. Even from a young age, when my friends were talking about growing up to be a veterinarian or princess, I knew that I wanted something more. I wanted a life that shined. I wanted something beautiful. My problem was, I never thought that it was written in the stars for me. I now see that I was wrong.

Let me ask you a question. Do you know someone who seems to live an extraordinary life? Maybe someone who always has amazing things happening to them? Regular people that you personally know in your day to day life, but they live a life that is somehow more?

I have known these types of people; people who really live and embrace life, and seem to be successful no matter what they are doing. These individuals feel like they have the secret to living a happier life than the rest of us.

I am here to tell you that the only thing that separates you and me from them is ourselves. You see, we tell ourselves these lies that we were just born into the lives that we have, or that the negative situations we are in are just luck of the draw. Lying has become something that we use as a defense mechanism so that we don't have to do the hard work that it takes to live extraordinary lives. These lies are also something that we can use to make us feel better when we feel like we have failed. When there is a missed opportunity that we never did anything about, we can just tell ourselves that this life is what we have been given; it is what we deserve.

I know from firsthand experience that you can, and you should, be able to live an extraordinary life. There is no such thing as luck. The people who are more successful are the ones who ask for what they want, and do the work. The key is to make small changes every single day in your attitude and the tasks that we are given. We must actively make mental shifts in the way that we see ourselves, the way we see others, and the way that we see the world. These small changes and mental shifts are going to have an extraordinary impact upon your life and will free you to live a happier and healthier life than you ever thought possible.

I was always certain that I was born to live an ordinary life. I convinced myself that I was nothing more than a "normal person" and that what I had was good enough. Not only was it good enough, it was as good as it was ever going to get. I had settled for a life of mediocrity.

It took the death of someone that had really made an impression on me to truly begin to understand the brevity of life. This person was Paul Walker. I did not know him personally but from every interview that I watched throughout his career to the way that his friends and family spoke about him, I knew that he was one of those people who seemed to have some sort of magnetism. He threw himself into everything that he did completely. He was generous, compassionate and loved with his whole heart. So many people loved him the same. Everyone wanted to be around him because he shined. He truly lived with purpose. It wasn't until a tragic accident took his life that I was given the gift to see how amazing life can be.

I finally stepped out of the fog that made me see myself and the world around me as something of shadow instead of the light that it is. I asked myself what I wanted out of life. I asked myself what was it about Paul that I had lost and those like him who live similar, impactful lives. What sets them apart from the rest of us? I came to the conclusion that these people are healthy physically, mentally, and spiritually. They are at peace with who they are. That healthy body, mind, and spirit affects how they interacted with others and the world around them, and allows them to live fuller, happier lives. I also realized that I want that freedom to be happy, and I was ready to do the work that was necessary.

To begin, I knew that if I tried too much at one time, I was going to fail. I started by making small changes each day to my physical health, my mental health, and my spiritual health. After only a week of these changes, I began to see the walls of my old self beginning to crumble, and a fresher, more vibrant me taking shape. I began noticing that these small, easy, and realistic steps were allowing me to see a clearer vision of who I want to be. For the first time in my life, I felt that I had a real purpose.

I know that if you go on this journey with me, you will feel better physically which will enable you to think clearer and therefore help you make the decisions that are the most beneficial to you. It will provide you with the confidence that you need to see yourself clearly as an individual. It will give you the courage to go after the things that you want but are afraid to chase. You are going to learn more about yourself and where you fit into the universe. Hopefully, it will help you find what your purpose is.

Because I have gone down this road myself, I know that if you can begin by making daily changes in your physical, mental and spiritual self, your perception of life will change drastically. In doing so, you will be able to live your life at optimum health, succeed where once you only found failure, find a sense of purpose, and live happier than you have even dreamed.

Today's Playlist

Break Free- Queen

Kanye- The Chainsmokers

Young Blood- The Naked and Famous

Today- The Smashing Pumpkins

Do You Realize? - The Flaming Lips

Alive- Sia

Into The Wild- LP

Towers- Bon Iver

Chapter 2: Being Found

When I began this journey, I was utterly and completely lost. I was negative, physically unfit, depressed, and lonely; the list goes on and on. I knew that I wanted something more out of life, but I wasn't sure what and I wasn't sure how to find it. It was around this time that Paul Walker passed away and I knew that I owed it to him and to me to live an extraordinary life. I went looking for ways to do just that. I began watching documentaries about the human body, and about the people on this earth who are said to be the happiest. I listened to podcasts at work on how to be productive, how to set you apart from others, and what makes for an impactful life. I started reading everything that I could get my hands on about achieving goals nd being successful. I read about the spirit and about miracles. I read about love. Through all

f this research, as well as the small changes that I continued to make every day, I began to see

uge shifts in the person that I once had been. Amazingly, the people around me were

ecognizing the changes in me as well.

My eyes were opened and I was able to understand more about myself as a physical

eing. I recognized the importance of exercising and providing my body with the fuel that it

eeds to keep it functioning properly. I noticed an amazing change in the way that my brain

orks when I supply it with proper nutrients. I am more capable of using better judgement, and

aking decisions that are more beneficial to me and to those around me.

I am more confident now than I have ever been or ever even thought possible. I found

e courage to go after the things that I want, and say "no" to the things that I don't. I have

arned how to stick up for myself and my beliefs. I have found new things that I enjoy that I

ever thought to try. I now know the beauty of getting out of your comfort zone, and all of the

agic that lives just on the other side. I have opened myself up to new opportunities, and not

rced myself to stay in the box of what I thought life should be. I have a fuller appreciation for

e and all of the amazing things that it brings.

The connection that I now have with God is unlike any other connection that I have. I

ave more of an appreciation and understanding for my higher power, and through that I am

ware of the way that all living things are connected. I have found the importance of other

eople and how we really cannot do any of this alone. Most importantly, I have found a calling,

purpose for my being present on this earth.

Life is short and with each day that passes, it is only becoming shorter. Do not let your life pass you by while you are on the side lines watching. Go out and do the things that you have always thought were nothing more than dreams.

I started this adventure of self-discovery to get more out of life and what I found was something beautiful. I want for every single person on this earth to find the same kind of joy, love, and peace that I have found. I want everyone to be the very best versions of themselves so that they can live the lives that they were meant to live. I want to help you take the first step by sharing my journey and my experiences with you through this book. I know that it will be worth your time. I believe in your journey and I know that you can live an extraordinary life. Namaste.

Today's Playlist

We're Not Gonna Take It- Twisted Sister

New Morning- Alpha Rev

On My Way- Rusted Root

Sound of Change- The Dirty Heads

Are You Ready (On Your Own) - Distant Cousins

Lose Control- Colony House

Keep Your Eyes Open- Needtobreathe

Water- RaRa Riot & Rostam

Your Physical Self

"The journey of 1000 miles begins with a single step" - Lao Tzo

Chapter 3: Let's Get Physical

We are going to begin this journey with everyone's favorite: our physical selves! (In case you didn't catch on, yes, there was a hefty amount of sarcasm there). What I mean when I say our "physical selves" is our actual person. Webster's dictionary defines the word physical as, "relating to the body of a person instead of the mind". Of the three parts of ourselves that we are going to focus on, this is the most important place to start. It is going to lay a foundation for the other two areas: mind and spirit.

It is no surprise that when we eat healthier foods and exercise our bodies more frequently, we feel better. This is because the food that we consume is what fuels us and helps our body to function. Think about a car. If you want it to drive as smoothly as possible, you are going to have to maintain it, and fuel it with the right gasoline in order for it to work at its optimum level. The same goes for the human body. If you want it to perform at peak condition, you are going to have to put more thought into how you sustain it.

Eating healthy is not the only thing that we have to take into consideration. Dreaded exercise is also going to be a key player. Even though it is not everybody's favorite, exercise is crucial! It improves moods, and helps lower stress and anxiety. In a medical article in *Healthline*, Ann Pietrangelo talks about the effects that stress and anxiety alone can have on our bodies. She says that it can prohibit your body's central nervous system, endocrine, cardiovascular, digestive, muscular, and immune systems from functioning properly. I don't know about you, but that sounds like just about every part of the body. If you knew that even walking for 30 minutes a day could help keep all of these bodily systems running smoothly, wouldn't you at least like to try? I know that I would.

I will give you some positive and realistic ways to get you into the best place physically Now that we have made peace with the fact that in order to live a much fuller life, we are going to have to make better choices for our bodies through nutrition and exercise, let's get started!

Today's Playlist

Human- Killers

Living Dead Girl- Rob Zombie

Game On- Pitbull, TKZee, and Dario G

Fire Work- Katy Perry

Sail- Devil Driver

2Heads- Coleman Hell

I'm An Albatroz- AronChupa

Try Everything- Shakira

Chapter 4: Music

I know what you are probably thinking. What in the world does music have to do with getting a body like the ones on American Ninja Warrior? Well, young grass hopper, let me spell it out for you. In an article in *Psychology Today*, Jacob Jolij and Maaike Meurs conducted a study that, simply put, states that music is capable of giving you the perception that something is inherently one way or the other. If you are listening to upbeat music when you are looking at something, you will be inclined to believe that it is positive. Whereas, when you look at the same thing while listening to melancholy music, you will perceive it as being a negative.

That being said, when you are preparing your life for a physical journey, don't you think you are going to want to make it as positive as possible? With the help of a playlist, designed with you in mind, you are going to be on your way to feeling better than you ever thought possible. Listen to these songs when you are out for a walk or decide to go to the gym. Play it on the days that you absolutely do not want to get out and get your body moving. It'll give you the kick that you need. Listen to it while grocery shopping for those healthier foods to keep you motivated for the life you are working toward.

You may have noticed a playlist at the end of each chapter. These are my personal motivators. When you are creating a playlist, it is imperative to keep in mind that it is only for you. Pick songs that speak to you and what you are looking for. Who cares about what songs are on there or what artists you choose from? If Mylie Cyrus gets you pumped up, then you go into that kick boxing or yoga class swinging from a wrecking ball (metaphorically speaking, of course). This playlist is all about you and your success. Forget about what other people are going to think about your music, or if it seems a little bit cliché. Make your picks and rock out to them all the way to the top.

Make sure that your music is accessible! Have it on your phone, your iPod, or in your car so that you can listen to it anytime, anywhere. That way, when you need an extra kick to get you going, you will already have that motivation handy. If you are like me, meaning stuck in the 90s, you can even make a mixed cd and carry it around with you. (It's still a thing; I do it all he time!)

Today's Playlist
Stricken- Disturbed

Waka Waka- Shakira

Strip Me- Natasha Bedingfield

Turn Down For What- DJ Snake and Lil John

GDFR- Flo Rida

Midnight City- M83

Madness- Muse

Wild- Troye Sivan

Chapter 5: I think I can, I think I can, I think I can

Something that I have learned to fully embrace (throughout my journey over the past

year) is the use of a great mantra. I used to think that mantras and affirmations were a little bit

silly, and I felt a little foolish using them. However, proper mindset is essential to making changes. What you put into your mind is what you are going to get out of it. If you are a little unclear about what mantras or affirmations are, I will clear them up for you real quick. Webster's dictionary defines a mantra as, "an often repeated word, formula or phrase, often a truism". An affirmation is defined as, "a statement or proposition that is declared to be true". It is saying something over and over to make it a truth.

Find something that is important to you, to your journey, and to your success. It can be something that you heard someone else say. It can be a quote or a scripture. It can be something that you create all on your own that you believe encapsulates what you are striving for. Whatever you decide, let it be true for you. I will give some examples of mantras that I love and have used myself.

- Genesis 1:26 –"Then God said, 'Let us make man in our image, after our likeness.'" I love this one because it reminds me that I am made in the likeness of God. It helps keep me from feeling discouraged on more difficult days.
- I Corinthians 6:19-20 – "Or do you not know that your body is a temple of the Holy Spirit... So glorify God with your body." I had read this over and over in my life, but it wasn't until I had decided to make a change for myself that I truly began to understand it. I stopped looking at my body as something negative and started to view it as something beautiful. This body that I am in, it is the only one that I get, and it is through this body that I am going to go and do great things. My body is a vessel that is going to be used to tell my story, just as your body is the vessel that

is going to go and tell your story. "My body is a temple, it is something holy." The more I said this to myself, the truer it became.

- I am enough.
- I went to a talk by a writer named Rob Bell and he had this whole idea of not comparing yourself and your story with someone else's. He continuously said **"What is that to you?"** in terms of what someone else is or isn't doing in their lives. I find myself saying this all the time when I feel myself trying to measure up to what another person is doing.

Again, these are some examples that have worked for me. Obviously, we are all different. That is part of the beauty of life. Choose what motivates you. Decide what your truths are.

The wonderful thing about finding a mantra is you can say it anytime, anyplace. You can write it on your mirror at home. You can put it on a sticky note and post it up at work. You can take a picture of it and put it on the background of your phone. Keeping yourself motivated is the best way to achieve optimum physical health, and your own personal mantras and affirmations will play a huge part in getting you there. When you say or see something continuously, it will eventually become so ingrained that it becomes part of your true self.

Today's Playlist

The Fighter- Gym Class Heroes

Want You to Want Me- Jason Derulo

Red Hands- Walk Off the Earth

Tubthumping- Chumbawumba

Shut Up and Dance With Me- Walk the Moon

The Man- Aloe Blacc

Electric Love- Borns

Promises- Nero (Skrillex Remix)

> In the shadow of your
> man made truth that
> breeds nothing but hate.
> Why the cold indifference
> for those were here to
> feed, to save. Won't you
> stretch out your hand
> and help up your broken
> brother? What does your
> heart tell you? Does it
> advise you to ignore the
> pleas or to extend
> Peace and now...

Chapter 6: Dear Diary

When I was a kid, I loved the idea of having a diary, and not just because all the girls were doing it. It was a way for me to keep track of everything that was going on in my very important 12-year-old life. It was a way for me to be able to look back and easily recall the entire goings-on in the world around me. We have all grown up since those days, but for the sake of your future self, we are going to bring back the journaling. Yes, I realize that keeping a journal is something that seems would only be popular among middle school girls, but the truth is it may be one of the most important parts of your journey and the changes that you have within your power.

Believe it or not, I am not the only person who would tell you that keeping a journal is something that you should do to aid in personal growth. Why, you may ask? It will keep you accountable. It is going to help you set goals, and will allow you to track your progress.

I found that it was exciting to get the ball rolling by treating myself to a new notebook dedicated specifically to create a new me. It doesn't have to be new, shiny, or expensive. Just make sure whatever journal you decide on is unused so that the whole thing can be focused solely on you and your transformation.

Open your journal to that first, pristine page. Take out the pen that is going to record the very details of your journey. These are the tools you will use to chart where you have been and where you strive to travel. Write the following question.

- Why am I embarking upon this journey of self-improvement?

Now answer it. Take a few minutes and write whatever comes to your mind. We all have our own unique reasons for why we want something different, something more. When you do this exercise, focus on this question only. Allow everything else to become nothing more than white noise. Let the words flow out of you to expose your truths. Maybe you want to live a healthier life for your kids or grandkids. Perhaps something has happened that has caused you to wake up and realize that you don't like the way you are living your life. Maybe you see the way that your genetics are working against you, and you know that in order to live a more fulfilling life later on, you need to make positive changes now. It could be that you just want to feel better. Whatever the reasons are, get them out of your head and onto paper, because once they're there, they may as well be set in stone. Having your goals written out will help you see a clear view of where you are starting, and the path to where you are going to go.

The next question to write is:

- What has prohibited me from reaching my goals in the past?

Make a list of what has come in between you and your goals before. Use this list to create a mantra for yourself. If time is something that has been a problem before, you can try a mantra or affirmation such as, "I have a busy schedule but I will take at least 30 minutes every day for my health and the health of my future self".

As you write in your journal, especially when creating new affirmations, use terms such as "can" and "will" as opposed to "might" and "try". Though all are viewed as positive, the first two are more definite. It will start out feeling kind of strange. I know, I have been there. However, as you continue to say these mantras and affirmations each day, your mind will shift, and it will become a truth to you. That is when things in life really begin to change.

Next, make a list of physical goals for yourself. Be sure to include a time frame. This is going to help you stay on track later. Having your goals written down is also going to be a source of encouragement as you begin to accomplish things on your list. You are going to find a ton of motivation from crossing things off, and inevitably completely the whole list.

Something that I have found to be incredibly helpful in the goal setting is to make smaller goals within the larger ones. Sometimes big goals can feel daunting, but if you can find a way to break each big goal into smaller goals, you will find it much easier to accomplish them.

An example could be that you want to run a marathon. The thought of just going and running 26.2 miles seems overwhelming. Start with the goal of running a 5k. You will still have to go through training to get your body into the appropriate shape to participate in the 5k, but at the same time this will be preparing your body and mind for your marathon as well. Once you have completed the 5k, you will be excited about the smaller victory. You will be motivated to try for something a little bigger like a 10k, and you will still be working towards the ultimate goal of the marathon. These smaller victories are a wonderful way to allow you to maintain momentum.

The last thing that I would suggest is that you sit down and write out what I call your "personal truths". These are the things that are out of your control and could frustrate you throughout your journey. It is important that you know these "personal truths" going in. They can help you make the right choices for your body specifically, and aid you in making a potentially difficult journey a little smoother with more direction.

An example would be genetics. If you know that diabetes or heart disease runs in your family, you are going to have to take extra steps to make sure that you are doing everything in your power to live a life that will prevent those diseases. It will help you find foods to eat or not to eat. It will tell you exercises to try or not to try.

"Personal truths" are the things you know about yourself because of who you are and he body that you were born into. They can be a possible struggle or something that you know ou are going to have to work harder at. Know what your truths are. Give extra attention to hose things that you will struggle with the most so you won't get bogged down later on by them. Face the struggles first and face them head on. Everything else will just be icing on the cake.

Today's Playlist

Fight Song- Rachel Platten

Unwritten- Natasha Bedingfield

Cheerleader- OMI

Arrows- Fences

Starlight- Muse

Lifeline- Papa Roach

Bangerang- Skrillex

Downtown- Macklemore & Ryan Lewis

<u>Chapter 7: Ready, Set, Go!</u>

Now that we have laid a bit of ground work by learning the importance of daily affirmation, finding music to keep us encouraged and motivated, and journaling to keep track of progress and chart our goals, it is time to take action. So what does this mean? We know what we are supposed to do to live a healthier life, but it all seems so over whelming sometimes. Here are some realistic ways to help you take action and formulate a way to do it and stick to it.

First off: detox! I have found it beneficial to do this literally as well as figuratively. There are numerous reasons why a detox is wonderful for you. Ridding the body of toxins which cloud your brain and prevent all of your systems from working to their optimum level is going to be one of the best things that you can do. This is going to give you a blank slate upon which to create your masterpiece.

Detoxing is something that seems just down right awful, but it doesn't have to be. The key is to find a detox that works well for you, and what you feel your body needs or doesn't need. You can go to a health food store like GNC or other supplement stores to find a good detox. You can find one that requires little to no money by doing a little internet research. I have used some detox methods that I found on Pinterest, and they were all gentle on my body and on my wallet. The best part of a detox that you make yourself is that you know exactly what you are putting into your body. If these suggestions don't suit your fancy, talk to a doctor. See what they would recommend to you. After all, they are the professionals.

Detoxing is something that I feel you must also do for your mind. When going into this new adventure- changing the way you think and the way you live- it is best if you take a little bit of time and declutter. Get all of the excess junk out of your mind and your personal living space. I always begin with a big cleaning day. Clean out the space around you. Throw out what is cluttering your world and doesn't have a purpose. If it doesn't have a purpose, it is nothing more than a possible stressor or distraction. Simplicity is the best way to destress your life and that is the type of mindset that we will be aiming for throughout this journey.

Next is what I like to think of as the "copycat". Think of someone whom you admire for their health and their physical lifestyle. It can be someone that you know in your day-to-day life or even a celebrity. This is a good time to pull out that journal. Write down what it is that you admire about this individual. Make decisions in your daily life that would emulate this person. What is it about them that speak to you? Is it the things that they are involved in? Are they a master yogi or a rock climber? Are they a serious MMA fighter and crazy tough? What is it about them that call out to your spirit? Try that! Don't be afraid to get a little messy and try a bunch of stuff. In fact, that is exactly what you should do! This is all about self-discovery after all.

People are going to be a wonderful resource for you. Find a person or a group of people who have similar mindsets and goals as you. It is easier to stick to a goal when you aren't doing it all by yourself. You will see that you are much more motivated, and have an easier time sticking to things when you have a sense of community. If you love to run, find a runners group. If you want to become a vegan, attend a vegan cooking class. There are so many tools available to us in this day and age that you will be able to find a niche for whatever it is that you are looking for.

Being dedicated to your new life choices can be very difficult. Sticking to a strict schedule for an exercise routine or trying to stay on track with a new nutrition plan can be a drag. Believe me, I know all about it. Remember when we talked about setting smaller goals to help you accomplish those small victories? Have something in place to reward yourself for those victories. I want you to be successful, and I know that you want that for yourself as well.

The truth is, however, that denying yourself those little pleasures is going to be a great way to find yourself running towards the road to self-destruction. Work hard, set goals, and stick to them. When you reach those goals, treat yourself!

When it comes to treating yourself for those small victories, don't use rewards that could create a possible set back. If you are trying to lose weight, pick a non-food treat. Bu yourself a new workout DVD or a new pair of running shoes to keep you motivated but also keep you excited about the great progress that you're making. As a writer, I have to set goals t keep myself on track. When I hit my desired word count or finish a particularly difficult section am working on, I give myself the gift of going to see a movie, an afternoon of binge watching Game of Thrones, or even a few hours of reading a fictional book, just for fun. No guilt, just a mental high-five for a job well done. I know when the credits roll, the Lannisters kill off my favorite character, and Harry finally defeats Voldemort, that it is time to get back to work!

I often find that the terminology that I use in life can be either a massive friend or foe. For example, the word "diet". I loathe the word diet. Celery immediately comes to mind, and t me, everything about celery is an abomination! I learned that when I made that mental shift and stopped telling myself that I needed to "diet", and instead told myself I was "making healthier choices" and "trying a nutrition plan", I had much more success than I ever had in th past. Words like "diet" have negative connotations that come along with them. Choose words in your daily vocabulary that are positive, and you will see those mental shifts making huge impacts.

Do your research on a new eating plan or exercise. Don't just go along with something because other people are or you heard from someone that it is supposed to be "all the rage". Read up! "Is eating a plant based diet healthier than one that involves meat?" "Is low carb more beneficial than counting calories?" "Is yoga better than running?" "What's the big fuss about CrossFit?" Go to the library and check out some books on different exercise routines or nutrition lifestyles that you've possibly heard about and are interested in. Find blogs or podcasts and see if these changes in your physical well-being are even something that will align with your personal truths.

One time I watched a documentary on veganism, and decided then and there I was going to be a vegan. (Well, I am one of those allergy people. That is a personal truth of mine.) I am allergic to just about everything but air and occasionally water. When it came time for me to actually be a vegan, I hadn't researched this new lifestyle. I only made it 6 days before I realized I wasn't getting the appropriate nutrients and hardly any protein. "Why?" because I am allergic to a lot of the foods that are used as replacements for animal products in the vegan diet. I have since read books, blogs, journals, etc. all pertaining to ways someone with food allergies, like mine can find the proper nutrients in a plant based lifestyle. You have to make sure that these life style changes are realistic for you. When you have invested your time, and many times money, into doing research about something new, it is much easier to stick to it.

Once you have recognized and accepted your personal truths, make sure that whatever you are deciding to do is something that is going to work for you. You know your mind and you know your body better than anyone else. Like I have said before, I want you to be successful at finding your best physical self, and part of that is making sure that you are choosing things that are appropriate for you. Do things in your success's best interest.

Sign up for something. A monetary investment is generally a fantastic place to begin. You have to go to your job(s) every day to make those paychecks and if you are anything like me, once those bills are paid, there isn't a whole lot left over. Using your hard earned money to invest in something is going to ensure you give it your all. I like to run. Maybe you do too. Signing up for a race is a great way to keep motivated, and that investment will give you an attachment to this specific goal because of what you have had to sacrifice for it. A personal trainer is also a great thing to have if you can afford it, but I know from personal experience that they can be costly.

Be accountable. This is the best way to make big changes. Stay accountable. Find someone in your life that can be your accountability partner. Check in with them once a week or every few days, and talk about your goals. Talk about what your stressors and setbacks have been. Talk about what your victories are. The key to this, however, is you actually have to keep each other accountable. You are "accountability partners" and not "mediocre partners". Don't let each other slack. We are in this to see change and make this life one that we are proud of. You have to do what is best for you, but make sure that whatever that is, there is a way for you to hold yourself accountable so that you can accomplish those goals and win those victories!

Today's Playlist

Sleep In- Telekinesis

Stressed Out- twenty one pilots

31

Numb- U2

Jungle- X Ambassadors

Despair- Yeah Yeah Yeahs

Geronimo- Sheppard

Ready To Die- Andrew W. K.

Another Story- Head & the Heart

Chapter 8: How to Keep Improving

I know from personal experience, when I start something new I am really excited about it. I am in it to win it, and I am prepared to make some serious changes. If you are anything like me, this zeal generally lasts about a week and a half and that excitement is gone. So, what do you do? How do you stay motivated to keep that fire lit?

Here are some simple ways to keep you going that I have found to be useful and keep me feeling positive about reaching physical health goals.

Be adventurous. Now I don't mean that you have to sign up to hike Mt. Everest or anything of that sort. What I mean is to try new things and go into them with an open mind. You can't fall in love with something until you have tried it. For example, I was always one of ose people who would go to the gym, put in 30 minutes on a treadmill, and then go home. ot only did I plateau in my progress, I was only using the same few muscle groups over and ver. I became unsatisfied and eventually quit all together.

You are going to have to change it up to get the most from your workouts. Don't always) for your first thought when it comes to cardio, endurance, strength, etc. If you want a cardio orkout, instead of hitting the treadmill find a Zumba class or try kickboxing. I personally love umba. It is fast paced and so fun that the time flies and you don't feel like you are working out. ow about strength training? The obvious choice would be to go and lift weights. There are so any other amazing options that I have found when it comes to building your physical strength. y some yoga or indoor rock climbing. These activities will help you build muscle but are also ntle on your body, unlike some other exercises.

Exercising can be something that you dread doing, or it can be something that you look rward to each and every day. Once I discovered that I love to dance, I look forward to dance asses like Zumba. It also happens to be a great source of cardiovascular exercise! I also love ga and Pilates for strength training. These are things that I genuinely look forward to doing. ey make my body feel better, and mentally, they are a huge stress reliever.

Find things that you really enjoy. You are going to have a very difficult time sticking to an ercise program if you hate it. Some people love to run but it is absolute torture to other ople. Don't sign up to train for a marathon if running is something that you detest. Chances e you are not going to make it through that program.

That all being said, make sure that what you are doing is good for your body. For example, one of my personal truths is that there are weak knees in my genetic history. I have to avoid things that I know are going to be a problem for me later in life. I enjoy running, however, I know that it is something that is very hard on the body, especially your knees. I try to do less of that and more of things that are more gentle on my body. I guess I should probably stick to the 5ks then, huh?

Commit to doing at least one thing each day that is going to make you a healthier person physically. This doesn't have to be something huge. It can be something as small as saying, "I am going to drink X amount of water today" or "I am going to go for a walk for 10 minutes after work" or maybe "I'll eat one extra serving of vegetables than I did the previous day". Rome wasn't built in a day, and I am sorry to be the one to tell you this, but your physical health isn't going to drastically change in a day either. It is going to take time. The key is to make tiny steps toward who you want to be physically each and every day. I promise you that you will get there and you will see results.

Don't let yourself get discouraged. It is easy to compare yourself to others. I still find myself doing it all the time! This is a tough one because it's just in our nature. I am here to tell you that we are all human beings. You are going to have days where you just need to have a cheeseburger and THAT IS OKAY! Give yourself some slack, enjoy the cheeseburger, and move on. You are doing the best that you can with what you have.

I think that it is also important to remember that even the most physically fit person that you know started at the beginning. They did not magically wake up one morning looking like Chris Hemsworth. Even Chris Hemsworth didn't always look like Thor. He had to put in a lot of time, energy, and money to be where he is today. It takes a lot of work to have that body that you want and the health that you are striving for. It takes a lot of sweat, pain, and sacrifice (by the way, I don't mean sacrificing food, I just mean maybe don't get two snacks at the movie!). This leads you to being someone that you can really appreciate because you know the long road it took to get yourself there.

Social media is something that can to be an invaluable tool. I use Instagram to follow people that I really admire for their physical and mental health. There are thousands of different people who post about their exercises or their recipes for all sorts of nutrition plans. You can customize your Instagram home page so there is nothing on there but positive inspiration for self-image, healthy and delicious recipes, work out routines to help you stay motivated, and exciting new things to try out. Facebook is another awesome tool that can be used for positive motivation, as well as accountability. Since Facebook is a little more personal than Instagram, you can share the goals that you are working toward, and keep people updated on your progress. You can even join various groups of people that are working toward similar goals, and you can use those groups as sources of encouragement.

I know that it is not necessarily realistic for everyone to be able to hire nutritionists and personal trainers. I am an ordinary person with an ordinary job, but even I have the means to try new things and stay accountable without having to put myself in debt. These social media sites are some of the best things that I can recommend to you for staying inspired and keeping yourself accountable so that you can really transform into that person that you want to be.

You are uniquely you and your body is a gift. As humans, we are quick to see the negatives about our bodies. I was this way for the longest time, and I would be lying if I said that I didn't still have these days occasionally. The thing is, however, your body is a vessel to help you accomplish everything that you are here on the earth to accomplish. Without the body that you inhabit, you wouldn't be able to do anything. Your body is a temple and it should be treated as something holy because it is the only one that you get. Respect it and treat it with kindness. Make choices for your body that are going to help it run smoothly, and won't cause it to suffer.

Today's Playlist

This Is Gospel- Panic! At the Disco

Starships- Nicki Minaj

Titanium- David Guetta (feat. Sia)

Teenagers- My Chemical Romance

Mary- Kings of Leon

Secrets- Mary Lambert

Waiting For the End- Linkin Park

My Body- Young the Giant

Part 2: Your Mental Self

"In the end, only three things Matter: how much you loved,

How gently you lived, and How gracefully you let go of

The things not meant for you."

-Buddha

<u>Chapter 9: Setting the Mental Sails</u>

Our mental self is the next part of ourselves that we are going to focus on. What I mean when I say our "mental self" as part of our life transformation, is our mental or emotional state of being. During this part of our journey, I hope that you will be able to come to terms with who you are, and can find comfort in who you are really meant to be as opposed to the person that you think others want you to be. We will also be talking about self-esteem and ridding your life of negativity. Your mental self is your true inner self and the place that all of your personal truths reside.

Like with any other journey, we need to make some preparations before we can set sail. We are going to start by doing a little unpacking. That's right! You read that correctly. We are going to get ready for this adventure by unpacking all of the negative and toxic baggage that we carry around with us. Believe me when I tell you that I know firsthand that this is so much easier said than done. We can't make any progress if we keep dragging around all of the negativity that pulls us down and causes us to derail.

When I talk about "toxins" in our life, I don't just mean the things that are obviously bad for us. A toxin can be as simple as a television show that keeps us from finding proper motivation. It can be a hobby that we love, but are spending too much time with it instead of on things that are going to make us better. A toxin in my life that I had a hard time facing was people. Let me explain this one. The people in my life that were often times toxic for me were people who I thought were my friends. They were people who I would spend time with, but when we weren't together, I would see how mentally draining they were. I would feel really bad about myself after the fact. Friends should be on your side, motivating you, cheering you on, and supporting you. I realized that whether they knew it or not, they found some delight in my failure. As a friend of mine once told me, friendship is not, and never should be, a competition.

I struggled for years with a handful of people like this. It was as though I was in an abusive relationship. They treated me poorly and it hurt. Then I realized the truth: I was the one that was in control of those situations. I didn't have to sit there and let them treat me that way or make me feel that way, and neither do you. Pick who you want to have in your corner, and make sure you pick people who are going to give you the support that you need to make this transformation. I am going to tell you right now, sometimes the people who end up being the very best for you are not the ones that you thought it would be. Don't let it get you down if your friends or family are not as supportive as you would have hoped. They are human too, have their own struggles to face, and are doing the best that they know how. That being said, there are always people out there who will be rooting for your success. All you have to do is be open to accepting them.

Another part of this is forgiveness. Forgiveness for you and for others is a must. You have to let go of the past in order to move into the future. I have learned in life that the only person who is hurt from holding onto pain and anger is you. The other person is not the one that is affected, but you will hang onto hurt and anger until you make peace with the situation and forgive. In the book *The Miracle Morning* by Hal Elrod, he talks about how we have to take responsibility for the situations in which we find ourselves in. It is the idea of blame versus responsibility. Blame is where you decide whose fault it is, and responsibility is where you decide whose job it is to improve things. In forgiving others, they may be the ones to blame, but you are the one responsible for forgiving the past and taking yourself to a place of peace and healing.

Sometimes, the person that you need to forgive is yourself. I saw a quote on To Write Love On Her Arm's Instagram that said, "I had to find forgiveness for the ways I hurt myself." Often we do harmful things to ourselves or put ourselves in toxic situations. We carry around the anger and disappointment in ourselves that prevent us from moving on. We know that we have done something harmful to ourselves or to others, but we will not accept what we have done and move on because we feel we don't deserve it.

My favorite poet, Tyler Knott Gregson, he has a poem that goes,

"Oh what we could be
If we stopped
Carrying the remains
Of who we were."

In the past, I put myself down on a daily basis. I made some bad life decisions and didn't let a day go by that I didn't remind myself. It wasn't until I started to become physically and mentally sick that I was able to step back and see where my self-hatred had led me. I was overweight, depressed, and exhausted from trying to run from what I had done. I decided I was tired of running and was ready to move from the darkness into the light. I did go see a doctor, and we decided that a small dose of an anti-depressant would be a good place to start. That medication, along with years of affirmations and reciting mantras of hope, love, and positivity, helped me break through the wall of self-hatred I had built. I slowly learned how to forgive myself and found a freedom that came from it. It is okay to forgive yourself. It is okay to let go of that hurt you have put upon yourself. You are worthy of forgiveness. You deserve a chance to be happy. That chance to be happy comes from within, and that all starts with forgiving yourself.

Today's Playlist

There Is So Much More- Brett Dennen

After the Storm- Mumford and Sons

Pursuit of Happiness- Kid Cudi

Life in a Northern Town- The Dream Academy

We Can't Stop- Mylie Cyrus

Vienna- Billy Joel

Water Me- FKA twigs

Jose Gonzales- Heartbeats

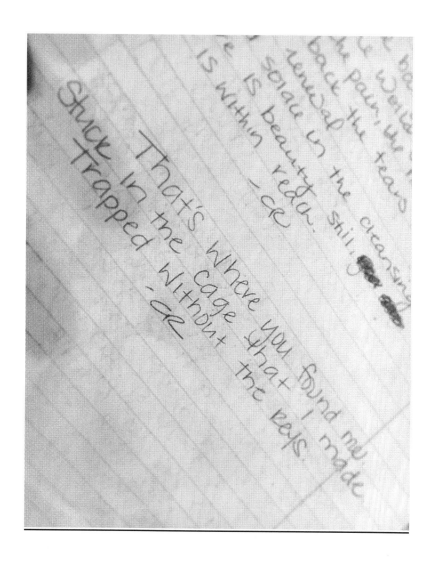

Chapter 10: Music, Take 2

That's right, we are going to talk about music some more. Like we talked about in the

physical health portion, music is so in sync with our moods that it is imperative that you fill your

mind with music that is going to uplift and motivate you to become the person that you want to

be.

Think about some things in your life that you would really like to improve upon. Do you wish that you had more confidence? Do you wish that you were a more forgiving person, a more loving person? Do you wish that you had the ability to attract a certain something or someone into your life? Find songs that deal with these issues and listen to them when you feel like you need a little something more. I know that the perfect song at the exact right moment in my life can completely change my attitude. Make sure you have that playlist already created and handy for when you need it most.

Today's Playlist

Kamikaze- MO

Peace Train- Cat Stevens

As We Are Now- Saint Raymond

She Always Takes It Black- Gregoy Alan Isakov

Ten Thousand Hands- Macklemore and Ryan Lewis

I Lived- One Republic

With My Own Two Hands- Jack Johnson and Ben Harper

Home- Edward Sharpe and the Magnetic Zeroes

<u>Chapter 11: Dear Diary, It's Me Again</u>

Back to journaling! Make a list of why you are embarking upon this journey of transformation. This is going to help you stay motivated when things start to feel difficult. I am sorry to tell you but there will come a point when you want to quit. Stick with it, I promise you that it is worth it in the end. Remember what is important to you, and use that to continue to push you forward.

Write down what is most important to you. It doesn't have to be one singular item; it can be a list of things. These are going to be the things that you are going to work toward. If you decide family is the most important in your life, then you know that everything that you are going to do throughout this journey is going to be for the benefit of your family. You will begin to make shifts where needed to spend more time with family. When making decisions, you'll make the choice that is most appropriate for your family.

When I began this journey myself, I talked with my dad about the person that I wanted to become. He told me to make a list of attributes that I wanted to possess. They can be big things or little things, but write down all qualities that are important to you and to the production of the person that you want to become. My list had things on it like: be caring and compassionate, be gentle with the earth, be kind to my body, fuel my body properly, eat more for sustaining and not as much for pleasure, shop from companies that give back, be grateful, be gracious and humble, stand out, care less about what others think, give myself a break, and shop locally.

As you can see, there isn't anything on my list that said cure cancer, solve world peace issues, or anything outrageous. My list contained things that I could make decisions on each and every day to take steps in the right direction to become that person I envisioned. This is your goal. Make small choices every day that will create the person you are striving to be. The wonderful thing about having them all written down is that you can go back to the list from time to time to remind yourself, see how far you've come, or add new things to your list.

Find someone that really inspires you or someone that you really look up to for the kind of person that they are. Emulate the way that they live.

- What is it about this person that resonates with you?

- What is it about them that set them apart?

- What are some things that they are doing that you can also do?

I have friends who are "ordinary" people, yet they seem to be living a life that is somehow more. They are happier and find more enjoyment in life. I wanted to know what it was that made them that way, so, I asked. I wrote them and asked what advice they would give to people who wanted to live better lives; what things they did, and how they got to where they are now. I got a random spattering of answers, but some of the things that struck me the most were:

- You are going to have to be okay with not always being comfortable.

- Ask for what you want.

- Be a part of life, not a spectator.

- See life for what it is, and not through different lenses. Lenses meaning how other people think you should see the world, how religion says you should see the world, or how your heart says you should see the world. These lenses aren't necessarily a bad thing, but you have to decide if you are seeing the truth that surrounds you when you look through them.

- Learn to appreciate the world how you want to appreciate the world, and not how you are told by someone else to appreciate it.

- Simplify your life. Slowly begin getting rid of the things that you do not need. It is all just extra baggage, literally and figuratively.

After I talked with these friends about how to live this dream of a life, I sat down and decided what I could start doing immediately. I took out my journal and began to brainstorm. Then, I got to work.

Today's Playlist

Oh My God- Hollow Wood

L'amour at la violence- Sebastien Teller

Lightning Bolt- Jake Bugg

Good to Be Alive (Hallelujah) - Andy Grammer

Brother- Lord Huron

To Build a Home- The Cinematic Orchestra

The Sound of Silence- Disturbed

Lumineers- Cleopatra

Chapter 12: Ikigai

What would you do in your life if you knew that you wouldn't fail or seem crazy to other people for doing? Are there gut feelings that constantly nag at you? Pay attention to these feelings because they could be an indication of the life that you are meant to live.

Pull out that journal. What blocks you from having your dreams come true? Make a list of each of these dreams, and then list the realistic ways that you can start making those dreams reality. If you feel like you were meant to be a singer, go to open mic nights, write music, or record a song. With today's technology, all you need is a smart phone to record your own music and create mixes. You can take tiny steps toward making those dreams come true, but take the steps. Your dreams can come true but nothing is going to happen if you don't make that first move.

Make a vision board! I love the idea of a vision board. Get some poster board, magazines, stickers, scissors, and glue, and prepare to get creative. Cut out pictures, words, or phrases from the magazines that inspire you. Glue them onto the poster board to make a physical representation of the goals you want to achieve and the person you want to become. One of my vision boards has things like travel, giving back, loving myself, and being healthy. Once it has been created, hang it somewhere at home or at work so that you can see it all the time. It is going to be a reminder for you to go after the things that you want, and to take the paths that are going to lead you to the person that you are becoming. I have mine hanging right beside the door at home so that I remember who I want to be everyday as I enter the world.

Someone that I have really enjoyed learning from in my journey to self-discovery is the "spiritual life coach" Jordan Bach. He is an inspiration and has helped me learn a ton about the universe, God, myself, and where I belong here in the grand scheme of things. One concept that he introduced me to is the idea of "ikigai". Ikigai is the Japanese idea that means "a reason for being". It is in each of us to find this ikigai but most of the time it is through a deep and long search for self. I love this idea, and it has become a big part of my journey: trying to decide what my part is in life and what I am here on earth to do.

Look inside yourself. Decide what drives and motivates you. These are the things that could be the key to what your purpose is. Everybody has a purpose, and your occupation doesn't necessarily have anything to do with it. A wonderful book about finding purpose in life is called, *The Art of Work* by Jeff Goins. I would highly recommend it for anyone who is trying to find where they fit in. It covers a great deal about trying to find what you are meant to do, but it also helps with who you are meant to be.

If you are having a hard time trying to decide where you fit in, helping others is a great way to start. Find a cause that you can really stand behind and get involved. I love the organization, To Write Love on Her Arms. It's founded by a man named Jamie Tworkowski. The foundation's purpose is to bring awareness and hope to those struggling with depression, addiction, self-injury, and suicide. It calls to me specifically because I have struggled with depression and anxiety off and on for over a decade. They bring light to some pretty dark topics. They let people who also struggle with these things know that they are not alone, and it is not weak to ask for help. I find that helping out, even in small ways, to bring hope to those lost in the dark, has given me more purpose than I have found in anything else. I know these pains and struggles firsthand, and carried them alone for too long. Sharing this with other people who feel hopeless and lonely has been an amazing gift that has helped me heal many of my own wounds as I help others heal theirs as well.

Today's Playlist

We Are Here- Alicia Keys

Hollow Moon- AWOLNATION

The Wider Sun- Jon Hopkins

Good Life- Alex Boye

Sing Loud- Alpha Rev

Cecilia and the Satellite- Andrew McMahon In the Wilderness

Brick-Ben Folds

Ray LaMontagne- Let It Be Me

Chapter 13: Self- Esteem

After getting involved and supporting To Write Love On Her Arms, I learned that the best way to heal is to share. Share your story. Share the roads that you have been down. Share who you are and where you came from. Your story is key.

Every person has a story to tell and when you open up and share that story, it's going to cultivate growth and healing within you as well as within others. You never know what struggles people are dealing with all by themselves until they open up and begin to talk about them. The problem is that most people don't want to be the first one to show the chinks in their armor. It only takes one person to open up and show their vulnerability for others to follow suit. Be that person.

Whatever it is that you are struggling and trying to cope with, you are not the only one. When you hold it all in and don't allow yourself to express your feelings and experiences, you are only isolating yourself and making the situation worse. When you open up, and share your trials, you will be helping others have the courage to open up as well. This is going to give you validation and motivate you to continue to let go.

The very worst part of this is the first step: opening up. Most of us don't for fear of what people might think about us. For the first 26 years of my life, I was afraid of what other people were going to think of me to the point that I remained silent about who I was and what I deal with. What is it that we are afraid of? Showing our vulnerability and humanity? I have learned that other people's judgements are just that- judgements. They are other people's opinions and actually have nothing to do with us.

Anthony Hopkins once said, "My philosophy is: It's none of my business what people say of me and think of me. I am what I am and I do what I do. I expect nothing and accept everything. And it makes life so much easier." This is so true, and something that we forget all the time. What someone else is going to think about you is all on them. We are never going to be able to change what people think about us or whether people like us, but we have all the power when it comes to how we let those opinions affect our lives. Be proud of what makes you unique. Life would be boring and monotonous if we were all exactly the same. Dr. Seuss said, "Today you are you that is truer than true. There is no one alive who is youer than you." You were made exactly how you are and you were made that way for a reason.

I have found in life that the people who are the most judgmental are also the ones who are the most unhappy with themselves. The things that they find fault with in others are the things they find fault with within themselves. Know that when a person treats you poorly and does not appreciate you for the amazing person that you are, it is because of a deficit that they have. They feel if they put someone else down, it is going to fill that void. Well, that isn't true. The way to happiness is inside you, and by making peace with who you are.

Don't allow yourself to be a doormat for anyone. I spent years of my life being a doormat, and all it did was give people permission to treat me poorly and make me miserable. Learn to use the word "NO". It is okay to say "no", and often times, people will begin to respect you more for sticking up for yourself. You are also going to quickly learn how amazing it feels to be in control of your life, and it will boost your self-confidence. I struggled with this and occasionally still do. The first few times you say "no" are the hardest, but it will get easier.

Now that you are ready to say "no" to the things you don't want, it's time to ask for the things that DO you want. You are going to get passed by for something just because people don't know that you want it. When we sit back in the corner like a wallflower and see other people being picked time and again for something that we want, we get our feelings hurt and feel under appreciated. Those feelings will quickly turn to ones of inadequacy, all because we didn't find our voice and let people know what we want. Will you always get what you ask for? No, but you will get a heck of a lot more than you would if you never said anything. Chances are you will continue to feel down about yourself if you don't say anything about what you want. However, I can guarantee that you will never be sorry that you took the opportunity to stand up for yourself.

Always keep the things that you know prove to be difficult for you in the forefront of your mind. Make it a point to work on these things the most. For example, if you have a hard time sticking up for yourself, make a point to do that as much as you can. It will feel very uncomfortable at first but like with a muscle, as you continue to exercise it, it will become second nature. Remember to give yourself some slack as you are starting out when you find that you can't do something perfectly every time. You are human, and you are doing the best that you can. Use that as a mantra if you need to.

Today's Playlist

No One's Gonna Love You- CeeLo Green

If I Needed You- Andrew Bird

Skinny Love- Birdy

Something Great- One Direction

MMMBop- Hanson

Ai Du- Ali Farka Toure

La Vie En Rose- Edith Piaf

Rivers and Roads- Head & the Heart

<u>Chapter 14: Stay Positive</u>

Surround yourself with positive people! Their positivity and their light are infectious, and you will have no choice but to allow it to rub off onto you. You know the saying, "bad company corrupts good morals"? The same can be said about spending time with good company as well. If you spend your time with people who are naturally optimistic, you will find that you too lean towards optimism. Don't allow negativity to take seed. We are human beings and experience a plethora of emotions on any given day. Unfortunately, negativity can be one of them. The key here is to stop those negative thoughts before they have a chance to cause any damage.

I used to be a naturally "glass half-empty" type of person. I didn't mean to be. In fact, I didn't know that I was this way for the longest time until someone at work started calling me Eeyore. You know, the character from Winnie the Pooh who walks around saying "oh bother" and waiting for the next catastrophe to strike? Yeah, that was what my coworkers thought of when they talked to me. If that wasn't eye opening enough, I had a friend try to set me up with her son because she said we would get along great since we" both hated everything". That comment was the one that really got my attention. I started to wonder if this was really what my peers thought of me; I needed to make a change.

Around this time, I had gone to see my favorite band in concert. Their name is Needtobreathe and they have this song called "Something Beautiful". I had heard it probably fifty times before, but this one specific time I listened to it, and it was like listening to a completely different song. The lyrics aren't exactly about the thoughts that I began to have, but it struck a chord with me. I started to think that life is something beautiful, and even in the darkest times there is something positive to get out of it. I challenged myself to post something every single day for an entire year on my Facebook and Instagram sites for what I call my "something beautiful" post. In these posts, I find something from that day that I found beauty in. A lot of the time it is something ordinary or obvious, but there are times when something terrible happens and I use it as a way to prove that even through fear and pain, beauty can show through.

Throughout the year of my "something beautiful" posts, my brain began to shift. Instead of going straight to the negatives about situations, my mind would naturally look at something and try to find the good in it. Some days, it was extra hard to find something good and beautiful, but it was always there. Everyone has the ability to be a "glass half- full" person, but you will have to train your brain to think in that way. Since I began my year of "something beautiful", I am a much happier and more optimistic person. I am the person now that other people take their inspiration from, and you can be that person as well.

Because we are humans and have those random emotions, there are going to still be days when things seem a little grayer. Believe me, even I experience them, and I have them more than I would like to admit. The thing about these days, though, is you can get out of them! Sometimes you are going to have to "fake it till you make it" and create your own happiness. You know yourself and your mind better than anyone else. Have an emergency plan set for when you get a case of the blues and find yourself in a funk.

What does one of these plans look like? Well, we are all very different individuals so everyone's plan is going to be different. Put on your mental health music mix that you made. It was created for days such as this! Know those things that always bring you joy. Mine would be spending time with my nieces or going to see a movie. I hate to admit it, but exercise will almost always get you out of your funk. Go for a walk or a hike. Get yourself out of the indoors and immerse yourself in the beauty of nature. How can you feel down when you are in the mountains or sitting on the beach? Volunteer your time to help others in need. It is tough to feel sorry for yourself when perspective starts to set in, and you remember how wonderful you have it. There are endless things that you can do to get back to feeling positive. Find some things that work really well for you and pull one out when you are feeling down. Something that you could do is to have an actual jar with these ideas written on them and when you find yourself in a funk, you can literally pull one of these out to get yourself out of that slump.

It's important to remember that you are human and it's okay to have a hard day. It is even alright to enjoy a little pity party every now and then. Just make sure that your little pity-party doesn't turn into a Great Gatsby sized pity party. Have a down day, just make sure that it stays a day and doesn't turn into a down month. Rent a mopey movie, enjoy that Ben and Jerry's, and then move on. Don't let it become a habit.

One last thing about positivity: It is near impossible to stay positive if you are not being true to the person that you are at your core. Life can be tough and it is even more difficult when you are trying to be someone that others want you to be, as opposed to who you really are. Remember your personal truths, the things that you believe with your whole heart. Stick to those truths and allow them to be your compass. Do not be ashamed of who you are. You are you for a reason. Embrace it!

Today's Playlist

Pennies from Heaven- Billie Holiday

What about Everything? - Carbon Leaf

Bittersweet Symphony- The Verve

Heaven- Brett Dennen

Everybody's Free (to Wear Sunscreen) - Baz Luhrmann

Empty- Ray LaMontagne

We Have a Map of the Piano- Mum

Of Monsters and Men- King and Lionheart

I'm not lost. I was never lost.
I was just searching, wandering.
At war for the truth that lies beneath the surface. The surface
which tells us beautiful lies of what we think we want and we
think is real.
Listen closely for the whispers of the unheard. Remove the
lenses of that dream which was never attainable and see the
unseen.
Find your way to the battleground. The map is buried deep
inside of you with the rest of the things you try to deny.
There you will find me bloody from the fight. Broken from
trying to love wholly. Bruised from mending the hurt.
Exhausted from clear vision.

Chapter 15: Rejuvenation

Taking time out for yourself each and every day is one of the most important things that

you can do for yourself. You will not be able to take care of others or your responsibilities if you

are not taking care of yourself first and foremost.

Find things that make your spirit come alive. You will know these things when you

experience them, and they are different for each person. These are the things that make you

happiest and are in alignment with the person that you are becoming. Just like with the music that we put into our mixes, these activities are things just for you. Do not worry about what other people will think about you doing them.

Express yourself and the person that you are meant to be. You can do this through writing. You can write in your journal or start a blog. You can do this through singing or dancing. Join a yoga class or practice Tai Chi. Maybe art is something that you are passionate about. Spend a while each day painting or sketching. Do something each and every day just for you to allow you to unwind and recalibrate your mental state.

Something that I have recently discovered is the idea of The Miracle Morning. The Miracle Morning began as a book by Hal Elrod. The idea is this: get up early and begin your day by doing what are called "Life Savers". These "Life Savers" will mentally prepare your mind for the day as well as help you cultivate a more productive and beneficial life. The letters in the word "savers" each stand for something different that you should do each morning.

S-Silence or meditation

A- Affirmations or those mantras we talked about earlier.

V- Visualization or actively picturing the things that you want most and seeing yourself obtaining them.

 E- Exercise your body to keep you in better health physically to be able to live your life to the fullest.

R- Reading things that are going to promote positivity and encourage self-growth.

S-Scribe or as I have been calling it, journaling.

Hal had the idea that if you would get up each day an hour earlier than you have to and go through these six things, huge changes will begin to happen within your life. This will also allow you time in the mornings to mentally prepare for your day and help you feel less stressed as you face the day ahead. It allows you to become a more productive person because you make giant strides in your life each day before your day really even begins.

Keep things in perspective. Often times we begin to feel fatigued by the ups and downs of our everyday lives. Be aware of how incredibly blessed we are. It is difficult to feel down when you are actively keeping life in perspective. Pull out your journal each night and write down three things that you are grateful for. Do this for a week and you will see how much of a impact this simple act can have both on your life and your view of the world around you.

There is a practice that I have been doing for a while that I call the "mirror test". Each night as I go to brush my teeth and wash my face in preparation for sleep, I will look at my reflection in the mirror and ask how I view myself as a person at the end of the day. Did I do something to impact someone's life for the better? Did I do something that held worth? Am I at peace with the way I portrayed myself and with the actions that I took throughout the day? How about how I treated others? I ask if I am content with the way I treated myself. If I look at myself in the mirror and have to answer negatively about any of these questions, I decide what I can do the next day to improve. I forgive myself for struggling during the day and go to bed grateful for the day I had, and promise myself to try harder tomorrow.

Letting go of the reins is one of the most freeing things that you can do for yourself. Allow life to unfold before you and sit back and enjoy it. Too often we feel that we need to micro-manage every little detail about our lives. Sometimes we are too focused on making sure what we are doing is perfect that we cannot see the amazing things that God has planned for us. Life is going to work out exactly as it is supposed to so relax; enjoy the journey.

Today's Playlist

Teardrop- Massive Attack

The Fear You Won't Fall- Joshua Radin

Razor- Foo Fighters

The Light- Disturbed

Tango Shoes- Bif Naked

Golly Sandra- Eisley

Check Yes Juliet- We the Kings

My Silver Lining- First Aid Kit

Chapter 16: Continual Growth

Just like with our physical lives, we have to be constantly growing our mental lives. I have found that the best way to grow and to avoid stagnation is to try some new things. They say that life happens right outside of your comfort zone. I have found this to be truth. When I began my journey, I always thought that I was an open minded and adventurous person. Well, was as long as those adventures still fit within the box.

It wasn't until became like Jim Carry in the movie "Yes Man" that I really understood th meaning. I had to train my mind to say the word "yes" to new ideas. There have been things that I have tried that I have found that I love, and some that I now know are not for me. For example, I found that I love to write poetry. I didn't know that about me before. I have always loved reading, and the idea of writing but poetry... that was a different story all together. I thought that it was insanely boring and confusing, but I tried it out and am now in love with it, and all of the ways that you can use it as expression. I also thought that because I love all art forms, I would really enjoy a figure drawing class. I was wrong- terribly, terribly wrong. It only took me about 2.3 minutes into that real life figure drawing class for me to realize that I was completely out of my element. Let me tell you, the last 118 minutes of that class crawled by. Drawing is not a forte of mine, and I have the "sketches" to prove it. What I learned, though, from these new things that I tried out was that when you get out of your comfort zone, you allow new room for growth. You will be surprised at the new things you find you cannot live without.

Read! Learn! Discover! I know that reading is not for everyone, so try out some audiobooks. Find material that involves things that you are struggling with in your life or topics that you are interested in. I have read numerous books in the past year that have played a major role in the person that I am today. Be open to new ideas, even when they seem scary at first. I was raised with a very conservative upbringing, and so some of the things that I have discovered about myself, and the way I see the universe now, have been scary. They are also incredibly beneficial, impactful, and have shaped the person that I am now.

Research topics that you are interested in learning more about and attributes that you want to possess. If you want to be a kinder, more compassionate person, read a book about humanitarians or Buddhism. Even if you are not a Buddhist, there are so many ideas and concepts that you can weave into your life and the person you are becoming. If you want to be a more successful person, check out Hal Elrod, one of the most inspiring success stories I've ever heard, or entrepreneur Lewis Howes, and learn all about their journeys. When you put your time and energy into doing the research, you are going to form an attachment. That attachment is what is going to stick and help create those changes within you.

Allow the universe to open doors for you. Keep your eyes open to new things, whereas before you would have been closed to new ideas, or not seen them for what they are in the first place: opportunities for new adventure and new growth. Allow the world to speak to you. Trust in your gut instinct and don't let yourself get in the way of your positive change. I know that there are times when we want something to happen, but because we feel that they aren't realistic possibilities, we don't see all of the ways the universe is creating avenues for those exact things. Once again, let go of some of the control and let life happen.

The world works in mysterious ways and when you sit back and just enjoy it, you are going to be amazed at where it will lead you. I was at a Needtobreathe concert and I had recently finished reading the book that their bass guitarist, Seth, and his brother, Chandler, wrote about going after your dreams. After this book, my whole life had been sent into a whirlwind of possibility. From their book, "Breaking Out of A Broken System", I found my way to another one of Chandler's books that created a need in me for something more, and the determination to go after it. Let's just say that Seth and Chandler Bolt have played quite the role in motivating me, and encouraging me to become who I always wanted to be.

Back to the concert. I was just coming through the security line when I looked up and there stood Chandler Bolt, the inspiring and motivating author, and I knew that I had to go and talk to him! So, being the complete fangirl that I am, I walked over to him and introduced myself. I told him how much of an impact he has had on my journey to becoming the best possible version of me. I was insanely nervous and I doubt a fourth of what I said to him made sense, but the thing is, had I not been on this journey, that opportunity wouldn't have arisen. He may have still been there all along and I may still have seen him going through security, but I never would have had the courage to speak to him. Since my eyes were open to new opportunities and I believed in myself, I had the courage to do something that before would have been unimaginable. You can too.

I found that when you find someone that you really connect with mentally and find inspiration from; they generally surround themselves with more people like them. I have a list of new authors who I have learned a great deal from. These authors have directed me to other authors and have been guests on podcasts and in different news articles. They have then sent me somewhere else to where my world has been opened up to many more individuals who have now helped lay the groundwork for the person I am choosing to be. We are all links in a chain and are all connected. You just have to be open to finding the best way to create the chain around you.

To end our section on our mental and emotional health, we will finish up like we did for our physical health by doing one thing each day to make you a better person mentally. This will ensure that you are making progress and taking steps towards that person you have inside of you who is happier and healthier. Personally, I enjoy meditation. I like to end my day by releasing all of the built up stress and worry from the day. I also spend time writing every day, even if it's just for a few minutes here and there. Finding a release through expression and creating something new has proven to be a great way for me to find mental peace. The "something beautiful" posts I make every day also ensure that I am keeping my eyes open throughout the day for the beauty that surrounds us.

One quick note about mental health before we move on. When surrounding yourself with positivity and trying to make beneficial changes can't seem to get you out of that funk and you find yourself in a real depression, it is okay to ask for help. Like I talked about earlier, I am someone who knows how it feels to be isolated by my own mind. I know that your brain can tell you things that are untrue, but at the time you can't see it that way. You aren't alone and there is always help. To Write Love on Her Arms is a wonderful organization for finding hope. Their website is TWLOHA.com. There are also suicide prevention hotlines as well as other resources. It isn't weak to seek help, but know that we all have a purpose here on this earth and the world would not be the same without you in it.

Today's Playlist

Porcelain- Moby

Young and Beautiful- Lana Del Rey

Life Is Beautiful- Vega4

Wake Up- Arcade Fire

Laundry Room- The Avett Brothers

Born Again- Josh Garrels

All I Want- Kodaline

Sleep On the Floor- Lumineers

Part 3: Your Spiritual Self

"The most astounding fact is the knowledge, that the atoms that comprise life on Earth; the atoms that make up the human body are traceable to the crucibles, that cooked light elements into heavy elements in their core, under extreme temperatures and pressures. These stars, the high mass ones among them, went unstable in their later years. They collapsed and then exploded, scattering their enriched guts, across the galaxy. Guts made of carbon, nitrogen, oxygen, and all the fundamental ingredients of life itself. These ingredients become part of gas clouds, that condense, collapse, form the next generation of solar systems stars with orbiting planets and those planets now have ingredients for life itself. So tha when I look up at the night sky, and I know that yes, we are part of this universe, we are in this universe, but perhaps more important than both of those facts is that the Universe is in us. When I reflect on that fact, I look up. Many people feel small, because they're small and the Universe is big, but I feel big, because my atoms came from those stars. There is a level of connectivity. That's really what you want in life, you want to feel connected, you want to feel relevant. You want to feel like you're a participant in the goings on of activities and events around you. That's precisely what we are, just by being alive"

-Dr. Neil deGrausse Tyson

Chapter 17: Third Time's a Charm

I know, I know, this sounds crazy. It's not, I promise you. What I mean when I say your spiritual self is how your spirit relates to others, the universe and/ or to a higher power. Let's start by making a playlist. You've seen a lot of my favorites throughout the course of this book. What are some of yours? Think of the kind of person that you want to be, and how you relate to other people and to the world around you. Find songs that speak to you on that level; songs that generate healing and a desire for something bigger than yourself. Let these songs be songs that you absorb into who you are at your very core; songs that when you hear them, you feel that they were written just for you.

Today's Playlist

Oceans- Hillsong

Love Song- Brandon Heath

Multiplied- Needtobreathe

Love Alone Is Worth the Fight- Switchfoot

Torn Apart- Judah & the Lion

Flawless- MercyMe

Come to the River- Rhett Walker Band

Peponi (Paradise) - The Piano Guys

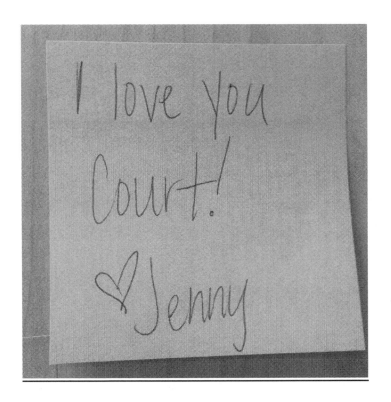

Chapter 18: Ask and Ye Shall Receive

"God grant me the serenity

To accept the things I cannot change;

Courage to change the things I can;

And wisdom to know the difference."

-Reinhold Niebuhr

Begin this portion of your journey by being prayerful and meditative about the path that

you are about to travel. Ask for guidance and direction. Ask for peace in all things, especially the

peace to relinquish control in order to fully find your purpose. Ask for understanding and clarity. Ask for courage to be able to stand out and stand up for your truths and what you believe in. There will be some soul searching taking place and you may be finding answers to some difficult questions. Ask for peace in regards to those answers.

Sometimes I find it hard to stay focused when I am praying or meditating on something. I find that if I use a journal to write down my thoughts, I am able to stick with it and my time is used more beneficially. While you're journaling, ask yourself the question,

- "What do I believe is the point of it all?"

I know that this is a huge question and one that you may not really know the answer to yet. That is okay. Hopefully as you go on this journey, you will begin to have your eyes opened to new possibilities, and have a clearer understanding of what life is all about. When trying to answer this question, make sure that you are answering it for yourself from your core personal truths, and not from what you think you should be answering based on anyone else's views. This journey is all yours, and one that you are going to have to weed through all on your own.

Ridding your life of distractions is like detoxing your spirit. Pay attention to the things that are fueling your mind. What are you watching on television or what kind of music have you been listening to? What about the books you read? Are these things adding to your character or taking away from it? The phrase goes, "you are what you eat". That goes for how you feed your soul as well. If you are pumping garbage into your brain, guess what is going to come out of it. Get rid of all of the stuff that is not helping you promote positivity.

Like with our mental health detoxification, some of the things that we need to look at getting rid of it are things that are not necessarily bad things, but are still harmful for our growth. Some of the people that we spend time with could be our friends and family, but the fact that we have such a hard time seeing eye to eye on big spiritual issues can cause adversity. You don't have to cut all these people out of your life but it is good to limit your time and involvement, and have a clear understanding of where your beliefs lie. Stick to them. Stay true to who you are and what you believe. The key to spending time with people that you don't completely agree with is respect. Be able to have a mutual respect with the people that have different thoughts and beliefs than you do. I have a friend who is an atheist, where as I am spiritual. She once told me that the difference between adversity and growth is respect.

I used to be someone who saw all the latest movies and kept up with all of the celebrity gossip. I always knew who was dating whom and who was related to whom. I knew all about the roles that they were in and all of the drama that went with the business. This in and of itself was not a problem. The problem was that I spent my time and energy on Hollywood, and didn't spend any on things that I should have focused on. It got to a point where I wouldn't know anything going on in politics or world news. I kid you not, I didn't know for days when Hurricane Katrina struck. I had become completely out of touch with reality. You see, there isn't anything wrong with enjoying the entertainment industry. That is why it's there. It is when you are so wrapped up in something that should be no more than a hobby, that you forget about human beings around the world who are hurting and in need. It is when you forget to be kind and compassionate that you need to take a step back and reevaluate your life.

The entertainment industry was just one of the examples from my life; it can be any number of things that is prohibiting you from being the person you feel compelled to be. Don't let yourself become so distracted that you forget what is important to you.

Once I realized how I had allowed myself to be distracted, I almost completely stopped watching any sort of television or movies. I strongly monitored the content of the music that I was putting into my mind and the sort of books that I was reading. I began to see how short life really is and I saw that if I was going to take the time to sit down and read a book, I was going to make that time count. This is when I started reading books that were going to help shape me into who I wanted to be. I wanted to be someone who knew more about what was happening in third world countries and less about keeping up with the Kardashians. I wanted to be someone that I could be proud of at the end of the day, and I knew that in order for that to happen, I was going to have to make some changes in what was and what was not important to me.

I am not saying that you need to be as rash as I was about the things that I was doing, but I found that in the beginning, it helped to take those drastic measures. When you cut out all of the excess, you begin to imagine what a life that is wholly focused on what matters would look like.

Knowing that you are not alone and that there is someone else in alignment with your future self is a wonderful way to stay on course. Actively seek to find a soul mate. Now, don't freak out. I know what you must be thinking. "I did not sign up for advice on my love life". Well that's good because I am not going to give you any.

I always thought that a "soul mate" was a romantic concept until the last year when I threw myself head first into this spiritual journey. A soul mate is nothing more than a person whose soul speaks to yours. It has nothing to do with any sort of romantic or sexual relationship. It has everything to do with someone who is in alignment with everything that you are in terms of the universe. These are the type of people that you want to have in your corner. These are the people who are going to be your biggest cheerleaders. Unfortunately, there isn't some sort of magical trick to your finding someone like this, but when you meet them, you will know. In fact, you may already have someone in your life like this. If you don't, remember to keep an open mind because the person who could be your most important soul mate could be someone who you never thought you would have anything in common with. There is also no limit to soul mates. You can have more than one, so keep yourself open to the possibilities.

It is also important to have someone you look up to and can go to with questions and concerns. Have someone you can trust with the difficulties of your hopes and fears, and who can help you find where you are supposed to fit in. The spiritual part of this journey is maybe the most difficult because most of this deals with stuff that's beyond our control. It's often easier to control our mental and physical lives. Find a mentor and use them to help you navigate through this life.

Surround yourself with positive people. Allow their optimism to be contagious. Spend your time with people who radiate the qualities you want and are able to make better choices about life. I tend to struggle with anger, resentment, and bad language. I knew all of this before began my journey. I knew that in order to be someone who was full of peace, contentment, and used only positive, kind words, I was going to need to be strict with myself on that things that I participated in and the people that I spent my time with.

I am going to reiterate the importance of using social media as a tool. Fill your Instagram account with people who inspire you and help cultivate the person you are aiming to be. On Facebook, you can decide who you follow and who you don't. Only follow the people who are going to be infectious towards your positive changes and who will be an encouragement to you.

My Instagram is full of encouragers and spiritual teachers like Jordan Bach, Jamie Tworkowski, Bob Goff, Rob Bell, and Tyler Knott Gregson. These are people who I would consider to be soul mates of mine. People who, when I read the things they post or hear them on podcasts or in interviews, I connect with all the way to a molecular level and I feel it in my core. The words they use to express themselves speak to me like an awakening that breeds truth within. This is what you are aiming for.

Brainstorm some things that you believe to be spiritual truths. Use them as guidelines for this journey. It is important to stay open minded but you also need to recognize your limits. Don't do things that go against what you know to be true.

Today's Playlist
Where I Belong- Switchfoot
How He Loves- David Crowder Band
Slumber- Needtobreaththe
Find Your Way Back- Foolish Things
Be Still- The Fray
True Love- Phil Wickham
How Can It Be- Lauren Daigle
The Cello Song- The Piano Guys

81

Chapter 19: Get the Ball Rolling

Begin each morning with prayer, devotional and/ or meditation. If you decide to give the Miracle Morning a try, this will already be a part of how you will begin each morning. Starting our day in this way is going to recalibrate your sense of being, and give you the knowledge of purpose and priorities.

Participate in random acts of kindness. Many people out there are lost and feel alone. When random acts of kindness are shown, it helps restore others' faith in humanity and most of the time causes them to pay it forward. Albert Einstein once said, "The most important decision we make is whether we believe we live in a friendly or hostile universe." Do what is in your power to make it a friendly universe. There can't be a thing as too much kindness. Selfishly, it feels good to make others feel good. Spread the love.

Practice authenticity. When you say that you are going to do something, do it. One thing that I have thought a lot about lately is when someone uses the phrase, "I will be praying for you". There isn't anything wrong with this phrase at all. Imagine you are the one to whom the sentiment is being expressed. Would it be more impactful is someone said, "I will be praying for you" or if someone asked, "Do you have a couple minutes right now that I can pray about it with you."? I would have to go with the second one. It shows genuine compassion and authenticity.

Do something for someone else and do it out of want, not out of obligation. There are people all over this world who are hurting and in need. The question is not, "what is going to be done about it?" The question is, "what am I going to do about it?" There is a quote by Mr. Rogers that I love. It says, "When I was a boy and I would see scary things in the news, my mother would say to me, 'Look for the helpers. You will always find people who are helping.'" Be one of those helpers. You will never regret showing compassion to another human being. There is a book called "A Course in Miracles". Some of the book's content goes way over my head and I would be lying to you if I told you that I have read it all and understand it completely. However, one thing that I have learned from it is the idea that you find your purpose through serving others. When you begin to feel a little lost in the world, start by helping someone else and go from there.

Spirituality can be kind of scary and daunting. I had to go about it through simplifying everything. I sat down and made a list of the basics on what I believe to be truth. Then I slowly moved out from there. When I got into things that I was unclear on, I knew where my journey needed to begin. I decided that I was going to stop believing everything that I have always been told at face value and learn it for myself. Like I said earlier in the book, I was raised in a very conservative community, and I have had to do a lot of soul searching to decide what is true to me and what is thought to be true by others. This all goes back to the lenses I talked about in the "mental self" section. I had to look at my spirituality as what was true for me without looking through the lenses of the community that I was raised in.

Once I had my truths narrowed down, I made a list of rules that I would hold myself to regarding what I will believe and what I will participate in. Does this seem like I have over simplified something as important as spirituality? Yeah, you bet it does. However, I didn't know how else to do it. I am great with a list of rules and following them step by step. The thing is, though, spirituality isn't that black and white, and so I had to create something for myself about what I believed. I figured out the basics and branched from there.

I have tried to remain pretty open minded about learning and accepting new things. Sometimes it is incredibly uncomfortable for me because it may be something that I was taught as wrong, but in actuality, it is just something that some people are unfamiliar with and that causes discomfort. Be wary of those comfort zones. As we discussed earlier, it is just outside your comfort zone that life awaits you. Keep your eyes open to new thoughts and ideas, and don't confuse discomfort with believing that something goes against those core beliefs. Make sure you really look into issues to see where they lie in those truths.

I used to hear about spiritual healing and spiritual teaching, and I thought that it was a bunch of crazy talk. There are still ideas about these spiritual teachings/healings that I am n sure whether or not they fit into my spiritual truths. However, they are an example of ideas I used to be very uncomfortable with and regarded as going against my beliefs. Energies, chakras, meditation, affirmations, etc. are all examples of concepts that I once believed held little value and didn't coincide with my spirituality. Once I came across Jordan Bach and Gabrielle Bernstein, as well as teachers like Marianne Williamson, I felt a mental shift. They expressed concepts in their teachings that I realized I agreed with. I also began to see the universe in a different light.

It is through these spiritual teachers that I am learning so much about myself as an individual, as well as a relational being, meaning someone who interacts with other people. I have learned that when you send love and positivity into the universe, it will come back to yo I have learned that when I am feeling a negative thought that I need to stop and ask myself "why?" Generally, my negativity is coming from something within myself that, once rooted ou I can find positivity and create a mental shift. It works every time. Just like my "something beautiful" posts, there is positivity and beauty to be found in all situations. Generally, all you need is a new way of looking at it.

Today's Playlist

Age of Innocence- Enigma

Fallen Embers- Enya

Imagine- John Lennon

Three Little Birds- Bob Marley

Thrive- Casting Crowns

Shoulders- for KING & COUNTRY

Devil's Been Talking- Needtobreathe

The Parting Glass- The High Kings

Chapter 20: Relationships

I have learned to realize that love is the only reality. Thoughts of love are the only thoughts that are true thoughts. When you have hurtful or hateful thoughts, they come from something within yourself that needs fixing. Keeping these things in mind has made a world c difference in my relationships. You begin to see people as people and become more patient with them. Aim to love more, truly love more. When you have that mental shift and start recognizing that people are human and doing the best that they can, you see that they, too, are on a journey of figuring out where they fit into this universe as well. Be gracious and empathetic. Life is hard.

On those days that it seems difficult to be positive and you find that you are thinking negative and hurtful things about people, ask yourself what the source of these feelings are. Do they come from fear? Maybe they come from jealousy or envy. There is always a reason that we are thinking these negative thoughts. Immediately stop those hurtful thoughts and make the switch. Once you have narrowed down why you have these thoughts and feelings, you can get to work on fixing the problem. If you are afraid that you are losing a person with whom you are in a relationship to someone or something else, stop and ask you where that fear comes from. Are you afraid that you are not good enough? If that is the case, you need to work on that part of you, and remind yourself that you are good enough and you are worthy of love. Fixing these inner issues is going to help you repair those relationships.

Be an encourager. You never know what battles people are trying to fight on their own. Just like you need to have comforting and encouraging people in your corner, other people need you to be the same for them. Have you ever been really struggling with something and received the exact right call or email from someone at the exact moment that you needed it? Or maybe you have something that has been heavily weighing on your heart, and you open a book and there's a perfect line that really resonates with you? I can think of more than one occasion when I was having problems with self-doubt and received a text message or a post on social media from a friend telling me that they were thinking of me. Knowing that I was not alone, that I had someone else with me who knew me and valued me in my corner, gave me the strength I needed to keep going. Be that person for someone else. It is impossible to live this life without other people. Make sure that the impact that you are having on other people is one that is going to change their lives for the better.

Jamie Tworkowski, the founder of To Write Love on Her Arms, once wrote something that really struck a chord with me. He said, "You'll need coffee shops and sunsets and road trips and passports and new songs and old songs, but people more than anything else. You will need other people and you will need to be that other person to someone else, a living, breathing, screaming invitation to believe better things." Someone is going to fill that position; let it be you. Be that invitation for someone who needs an encourager to let them know that there is something better.

Today's Playlist

Wedding Dress- Derek Webb

Out of the Woods- Nickel Creek

Glorious- Colony House

The Longing- All Sons & Daughters

All I Need- Mat Kearney

Dying Day- Brandi Carlile

Last Beat of My Heart- DeVotchKa

Sound of Melodies- Leeland

Chapter 21: Small Choices Lead To Big Changes

This may come as no shock to you, but I am going to tell you that the very best way to
ake big changes is by taking small steps every single day. Maybe you decide to perform one
ndom act of kindness each day. If you make that choice, even for a week, and those whose
es were affected by it also made the same decision, and so on and so on, can you imagine the
anges that would take place in this world? It would be astounding! Maybe you decide that
u are going to meditate for 15 minutes each morning or say one extra prayer. Whatever you
cide to do each day, do it for the health of your future spiritual self.

I have found when I fill my brain with information of attributes I want to have, I have a better chance of living those things. When I decided that I wanted to be a more loving person, I read books like, "Love Does" by Bob Goff, "Love Wins" by Rob Bell, and "Crazy Love" by Francis Chan. Fill your mind with positivity, love, compassion, and watch how it blossoms.

I have learned the importance of waking up each morning as well as going to bed each evening with a grateful heart. It prepares your mind in the morning, and gives you a positive attitude to start your day and carry you throughout. It will also help you in the evenings as you reflect upon your day and how incredible life is.

Today's Playlist

Fake Plastic Trees- Radiohead

Is There a Ghost- Band of Horses

Closer to You- Wallflowers

The Universe- Gregory Alan Isakov

Hoppipolla- Sigur Ros

I'm Gonna Be (500 Miles)- Sleeping At Last

Mess Is Mine- Vance Joy

Come Away With Me- Norah Jones

Chapter 22: What It All Boils Down To

I began my journey in search of the things that would help me become the happiest and ealthiest version of myself. What I learned along the way was that it doesn't matter what mily you were born into, how much is in your bank account, or what your business card says. ving a truly extraordinary life is all about perspective. It is all about being open minded to new periences and new ideas. Life is about being grateful for what you have and for who you are. ost importantly, living a life in extraordinary fashion is about kindness and compassion for hers, for the earth, and for you.

I still have the same job that I did when I began this journey. My family is exactly the same. I didn't pack up all of my belongings and relocate. For the most part, my surroundings have not changed, but everything about me is completely different. My whole life was turned upside down, and as I put my life back together, I was able to do it in a way where only important things in life have a place now. Life is incredibly short and it is only getting shorter. I refuse to waste any more precious time on shallow and trivial things. I will stand up for myself and ask for what I want. I will allow myself happiness because I know that I am capable of what is required, and am worthy of great blessings. I will treat myself and others with the highest love and kindness, and will seek peace in all things.

I encourage you to take the things that I have shared with you, the experiences that I have had, and go out in search of your own extraordinary life. Don't settle for mediocrity. Are you going to be able to take the easy road? No way, but as you find yourself truly enjoying the life that you are living and having the knowledge that you are on the correct path, you will be grateful for the rocky roads that you have had to travel. You will know that all of the struggles you have faced are bringing you to something beautiful. Namaste.

Today's Playlist

How It Ends- Devotchka

Over the Rainbow- Israel Kamakawiwo'ole

End of the Earth- Lord Huron

Windows Are Rolled Down- Amos Lee

Forever Young- Youth Group

Holocene- Bon Iver

Moonlight Mile- The Rolling Stones

Something Beautiful- Needtobreathe

Where I Got My Information and More

Chapter 2:

Documentaries I watched

- "Happy" directed by Roko Belic
- "I Am" directed by Tom Shadyac
- "Living On One Dollar" directed by Zach Ingrasci
- "Fat, Sick & Nearly Dead" 1&2 directed by Joe Cross
- "Food Matters" directed by James Colquhoun
- "Vegucated" directed by Marisa Miller Wolfson
- "Hungry for Change" directed by James Colquhoun

Chapter 3:

My definition of "physical" came from the online Merriam-webster.

There is an article that I read called, "The Effects of Stress on the Body". The article was written by Ann Pietrangelo and published online in *Healthline* on August 25, 2014. It was also medically reviewed by George Krucik MD, MBA.

Chapter 4:

I read an article that I found on the website, *Psychology Today* called, "The Neuroscience of Music, Mindset, and Motivation". It was written by Christopher Bergland. In the article, Bergland speaks of research conducted by Jacob Jolij and a student, Maaike Meurs, from the Psychology department of the University of Groningen in the Netherlands. The research showed the effects of music on our brain and how it changes out mindsets and moods. This article was posted December 29, 2012.

Chapter 5:

I used the online Merriam-Webster once again to obtain the definitions for "mantra" and "affirmation".

The scriptures that I pulled from the Bible (Genesis 1:26 and 1 Corinthians 6:19-20) came from the English Standard Version.

Rob Bell is an author that I have been inspired from for years. I had the opportunity to go to an all-day seminar in Denver where we all sat in a round and talked about his newest book. This book is called, *How To Be Here*. This book, as well as the discussions we had during the seminar, centered on how to live fully and purposefully while going through your day to day life.

Chapter 9:

Hal Elrod wrote a book called, *The Miracle Morning*. The purpose of the book is to encourage its readers to wake up with purpose each morning. Hal Elrod also has one of the most inspirational and unbelievable stores I have ever heard. He has a wonderful podcast called, "Yo Pal Hal" if you are looking for something to get you motivated and encouraged!

Hal Elrod is also discussed in chapters 15 and 16.

Tyler Knott Gregson is a poet from Montana. He is most commonly known for his Haikus on Love and Typewriter Series. Both can be found on Instagram and Tumblr. He is also the author of *Chasers of the Light: Poems from the Typewriter Series* and *All the Words are Yours: Haiku on Love*.

Chapter 12:

Jordan Bach is a spiritual teacher that I came across on Instagram, He is full of positivity, compassion and light. If you want to follow him on Instagram, his name is @TheBachBook.

It's no secret that I love To Write Love On Her Arms. As someone who has battled depression for years, this organization is a beacon of light. Their website is TWLOHA.com. It was founded by Jamie Tworkowski as a means to raise money to help a friend pay for treatment. Follow @twloha and @jamietworkowski on Instagram to learn more about what they are doing and how to get involved.

Jamie Tworkowski is also the author of the NYT Bestseller, *If You Feel Too Much: Thoughts on Things Found and Lost and Hoped For*.

Chapter 13:

The quote by Anthony Hopkins was found in an interview in *The Telegraph*. It was written by Sean Macaulay in January 2011.

Happy Birthday to You, a book by Dr. Seuss, is home to the quote I used about being yourself.

Chapter 14:

Needtobreathe is a band from South Carolina. Their song "Something Beautiful" is on "The Outsiders" album. If you don't know it, check it out. Check out the rest of their music while you're at it.

F. Scott Fitzgerald wrote a book that was published in 1925 called, *The Great Gatsby*. The protagonist of the story, Jay Gatsby, was notorious for throwing decadent but excessive parties. I think you can use your imagination on what a Gatsby sized pity party would look like.

Chapter 16:

Jim Carrey was in a movie in 2008 called *Yes Man*. In the movie, the main character, Carl challenges himself to say "yes" to everything.

Lewis Howes is a former pro athlete turned entrepreneur. He is most commonly known for his podcast, "The School of Greatness". In 2015, he published his first book

Seth and Chandler Bolt are brothers from South Carolina. Seth is the bass guitarist for Needtobreathe. Chandler is a bestselling author and entrepreneur. He is the founder of Self-Publishing School. Together they wrote the book, *Breaking Out of a Broken System* in 2014. This book was the catalyst for my transformation and I cannot recommend it enough.

Dr. Neil deGrausse-Tyson is an American astrophysicist. In an interview with TIME Magazine in 2012, he was asked the question, "What is the most astounding fact that you can share with us about the universe?" His answer is one that leaves me in tears. You can see the answer to this question at the very beginning of Part 3: Your Spiritual Self.

Chapter 18:

Instagram accounts I follow for encouragement and inspiration for my spiritual journey.

- @realrobbell
- @tylerknott
- @bobgoff
- @TheBachBook

Chapter19:

I found the Albert Einstein quote while reading an article in *Huffington Post*. The article was called, "Is It a Friendly Universe?" and was written by Liz Sterling, M.A. in August 2012.

Fred Rogers is most commonly known for his show, "Mr. Roger's Neighborhood" from 1968-2001. The quote about looking for the helpers originated in a video from the late 1970s in which Rogers advises parents on how to help their children during times of tragedy.

A Course In Miracles is a book that was published in 1975 by the Foundation for Inner Peace. It was scribed by Dr. Helen Schucman and is a self-guided book to help the reader achieve a spiritual transformation.

Acknowledgements

I want to thank my family for loving me just the way I am, quirks and all. My friends, who are chosen family, thank you for being in my corner. To all of my cheerleaders throughout this process, from the bottom of my heart, thank you! Your support and encouraging words are what I continued to draw strength from when I wanted to quit. To my lovely editor, Traci, for taking this book from the rough copy it was and helping me mold it into the masterpiece that it is now. I am in your debt. Thank you to my dad for the cover art. The face that you gave my book is exquisite. To Kitty at Lady Grey Photography for my author's photograph, it is magnificent. Thank you to everyone in the Self-Publishing School, I am eternally grateful that I found my way into your tribe. A special thank you to Mary, my accountabilibuddy because without you, these words wouldn't be here now. Lastly, to all of those who inspired me to take the leap of faith to find a life of "more". I owe you the most. Without you, I wouldn't be me.

29024758R00061

Made in the USA
Middletown, DE
21 December 2018